Python for the La... Conversational Guide to Effortless Mastery

Learn Python Without Breaking a Sweat

By Akselinc & StackFOSS

Python for the Laziest: A Conversational Guide to Effortless Mastery

Learn Python Without Breaking a Sweat

For permissions requests, contact the publisher at
contact@akselinc.com

Published by Akselinc & StackFOSS
www.akselinc.com
www.stackfoss.com

Akselinc: Nurturing Open Knowledge

Akselinc is a movement dedicated to nurturing open knowledge and innovation. With a passion for technology and a commitment to accessible education, Akselinc empowers learners and creators worldwide. Through collaborative projects and initiatives, Akselinc envisions a future where knowledge knows no boundaries.

StackFoss: Redefining Learning

StackFoss is a flagship initiative by Akselinc that redefines the way we learn technology. As an open-source powerhouse, StackFoss offers alternatives to mainstream platforms, fostering an environment of collaborative learning. By breaking down barriers and embracing community-driven education, StackFoss empowers individuals to navigate the tech landscape with confidence and creativity.

Content

Chapter 1: Introduction

Once upon a time in the digital world there lived a tribe of programmers. Some were tireless coding warriors, while others were known as the "laziest of them all." It's this last group that we'll focus on, those who have discovered the secret to success in the world of programming: Python.

The Lazy Path to Python Mastery

Welcome to the world of Python, the laziest programming language on the planet! If you've ever dreamed of becoming a coding wizard without breaking a sweat, you've come to the right place.

But wait, you might be thinking, "A lazy approach to programming? Is this even possible? The answer is a resounding yes!" In fact, Python is designed for people like you, those who would rather sip a latte than debug code all night.

Why Python, you ask?

Before diving headfirst into the world of Python, let's take a moment to understand why learning this language is a game-changer. Python is like a Swiss army knife for programmers. Its applications are as diverse as the characters in a great novel. From web development to data analysis, machine learning to artificial intelligence, Python does it all.

Not to mention, Python's syntax is so clear and readable that it's practically poetry for programmers. Plus, the Python community is one of the friendliest in the coding world. You'll find help, support and companionship every step of the way.

What's next for you?

Now that you're intrigued, let me give you a preview of the adventure that awaits you in this book. We are about to embark on a journey where learning Python is not limited to dry syntax and endless code snippets. No, it will be an exciting, engaging and entertaining experience.

Imagine yourself sitting by a campfire, swapping stories with a wise mentor who happens to be a Python guru. This is the atmosphere we are looking for. We'll use real-world examples, fun anecdotes, and relevant scenarios to bring Python concepts to life. You won't need to be a math genius or computer whiz to join this adventure; all you need is your curiosity and a pinch of laziness.

So, dear reader, get ready to embark on a Python adventure like no other. By the end of this book, you'll be coding like a pro, while enjoying the joy of doing it in the laziest way possible. Get ready for Python, served with a touch of humor, a touch of practicality, and a whole lot of fun!

Chapter 2: Meet your guide

Deep in the Python wilderness, where code snippets danced in the moonlight and variables whispered in the wind, there emerged a guide, a companion for your Python journey. Imagine, if you will, a character who is not just a mentor but a seasoned adventurer through the lands of indentation and syntax. Let me introduce our guide, Pyra the Pythonista.

Pyra the Pythonista: Your fellow coder

Meet Pyra, a seasoned Python enthusiast with a penchant for transforming the complex into the understandable. She wears a cape woven from Python documentation, and her trusty sidekick is a keyboard player who has seen more characters than a Shakespearean play.

Pyra's philosophy is simple: "Why complicate things when you can be lazy?" With a twinkle in her eye and a cup of coffee perpetually in hand, Pyra is here to be your fellow coder, your navigator through the world of Pythonic wonders.

A discussion near the virtual campfire

Now imagine yourself sitting by a virtual campfire with Pyra. The flames flicker as she regales you with tales of her encounters with delicate insects and the epic battles she fought with pythonic challenges. This isn't your typical programming guide; it's a conversation with a friend who happens to be a Python pro.

"Hello, fellow traveler!" Ready to embark on this lazy adventure? » Pyra would say with a smile. "Don't worry about the complicated jargon and syntax just yet. We're here to enjoy the journey, not stress about the destination."

The friendly Pythonic tone

As you explore the intricacies of Python, you'll notice that Pyra speaks a language everyone is familiar with: simple, friendly, and infused with just the right amount of humor. Concepts that might seem intimidating elsewhere become as accessible as a cup of hot cocoa by the fire.

In Pyra's world, mistakes aren't mistakes; these are opportunities for improvement. Variables are not simple containers; they are characters from our Pythonic story. And the curls? Well, those are the dance moves to the big coding ball.

Your conversation companion

Prepare to be guided through Python meadows and algorithm hills, as Pyra shares her wisdom, advice, and maybe a few coding secrets. This is not a solo expedition; it is an adventure shared with a companion who understands that the best way to learn is with a smile and a dose of lightness.

So take a seat by the virtual campfire, dear reader, and let Pyra guide you through the enchanting world of Python, where learning is not only easy but downright enjoyable. Get ready for a coding journey that's as friendly as it is educational, and remember: Pyra has your back!

Chapter 3: Python's lazy approach

In the bustling village of Pythonburg, where code flowed like a quiet river, the laziest programmers were celebrated as true heroes. Welcome to the lazy approach to Python, where relaxation is not only accepted; it's celebrated.

Embrace laziness in programming

In most fields, laziness is considered a vice, but in the world of programming, it is a virtue. Our hero, Pyra, believes that the lazier you are, the better programmer you become. For what? Because laziness in coding leads to efficiency.

In Python's lazy approach, we don't reinvent the wheel. Why write a hundred lines of code when ten is enough? Laziness here is finding the quickest and most efficient way to get things done. It's not about avoiding work; it's about working smarter, not harder.

The art of automation

Now imagine a world where repetitive tasks disappear with the wave of a Python wand. This is the magic of automation, and Python is your enchanting spellbook. Pyra, your fellow coder, swears by the magic words "Automate everything."

- **Repetitive tasks, no more!** Imagine never having to copy and paste the same block of code again. With Python, you can script your way out of the copy-and-paste madness.

- **Data Processing Wizardry:** Tired of sorting Excel sheets like a medieval scribe? Let Python's pandas library do the sorting while you sip your favorite beverage.

- **Web Scraping, the lazy method:** Extract information from a website? Don't worry about manual copying. Python's web-scraping tools will do the heavy lifting for you.

Lazy efficiency versus hardworking chaos

In the lazy world of Python, efficiency is king. Pyra will show you that it's not about writing more code, it's about writing the right code. Lazy programmers don't waste time on unnecessary complexities. They find elegant, simple solutions that get the job done without breaking a sweat.

By the end of this chapter, you will understand that being lazy in programming does not mean being unproductive; it's about being extremely efficient. Python, our trusty ally, is the lazy programmer's best friend, ready to automate the mundane so you can focus on the extraordinary.

So, dear reader, fasten your seat belt (or maybe just recline your chair a little), as we delve deeper into the lazy world of Python, where the mantra is "Work less, code more!" » Prepare to be amazed by the power of lazy programming and the incredible efficiency it brings to your coding adventures.

Chapter 4: Python Unveiled

In the ancient manuscripts of programming history, one language stands out as a beacon of simplicity and power: Python. As you uncover the story of Python's origins and evolution, you'll discover why this programming language is more than just a tool; it's a community, a philosophy, and a friend to beginners.

Origins: Guido's Gift

Our story begins in the late 1980s, when a Dutch programmer named Guido van Rossum set out to create a language that was both powerful and readable. Legend has it that Guido was a fan of the British comedy group Monty Python and so the name Python was given to this new creation.

- **Guido's Odyssey:** Discover the journey of Guido van Rossum as he embarked on the quest for a programming language that was both elegant and practical.

- **Monty Python Connection:** Learn how a love of surreal humor and the flying circus influenced the Python name and fanciful conventions within the community.

The Evolution of Python: From Crawler to Python Powerhouse

Over the years, Python has evolved like a chameleon, adapting to the changing needs of the programming world. From its humble beginnings to becoming the language of choice for tech giants and startups, Python's journey is a testament to its versatility.

- **Version Hopping:** Navigate through the different versions of Python and witness the language's growth from a curious project to a global phenomenon.

- **Pythonic Philosophy:** Discover the principles that make Python a language appreciated not only for its syntax, but also for its community philosophy and readability.

Python: the ideal playground for beginners

Now, why is Python the perfect starting point for aspiring programmers, especially those who might be characterized as "lazy" learners?

- **Readability reigns supreme:** Dive into Python's syntax, which is so readable that it almost reads like plain English. For beginners, this means a gentler learning curve.

- **Comprehensive Documentation:** Explore the wealth of resources available to Python learners. The extensive documentation and supportive community make Python an open book, ready to explore.

- **A versatile companion:** Whether you are interested in web development, data science, artificial intelligence or automation, Python is your versatile companion. It's a language that grows with you as you delve deeper into areas of programming.

The promise of Python to beginners

As you learn about the history of Python, you will understand that it is not just a language; It is a promise. A promise that programming can be both powerful and accessible. So, as we take our first steps into the Pythonic landscape, remember that you are not just learning a language; you join a community that values simplicity, readability, and the joy of coding.

Stay tuned, dear reader, as we explore the wonders of Python, a language that welcomes beginners with open arms and assures them that the journey is just as enjoyable as the destination. Get ready to embrace Python, where the code is clear, the community is friendly, and the possibilities are endless.

Chapter 5: Setting up camp

In our Pythonic adventure, before we can explore the lush nature of coding, we need to set up camp. In this chapter, we'll guide you through the hassle-free Python installation process, ensuring that even the laziest learners can embark on this journey with ease. Plus, we'll introduce you to the wonderful world of IDEs (integrated development environments) in a way that will make you want to write code.

Installing Python: A Step-by-Step Guide for the Laziest

Welcome, fellow lazy learner! The path to Python greatness begins with the easiest of tasks—installing Python on your machine. Follow these simple steps, and you'll have Python ready to serve your every coding whim.

Step 1: Choose Your Platform

Are you a Windows wizard, a Mac maestro, or a Linux sorcerer? Python loves them all.

- **Windows:** Head to the Python Downloads page. Click on the latest version, and you'll find an executable installer (.exe) ready to be embraced.

- **Mac:** For the macOS mavens, the Python.org website also offers a shiny macOS installer. Choose the version compatible with your system, usually the one labeled "macOS 64-bit."

- **Linux:** If you're a Linux luminary, you can either use your package manager (for example, `apt` on Ubuntu) or download the source code and build Python like a true coding artisan.

Step 2: The Lazy Installation Dance

Now, let's bring Python to life with a dance as lazy as a Sunday morning.

- **Windows:** Double-click the installer. Check the box that says "Add Python to PATH" (we don't want to hunt for Python when we're feeling lazy). Click "Install Now" and let the installer work its magic.

- **Mac:** Open the installer, and, much like casting a spell, follow the prompts. Don't forget to check "Add Python to PATH" for that extra touch of laziness.

- **Linux:** If you're using the package manager, summon Python with a command like `sudo apt install python3`. If you're venturing into building from source, follow the README—you're on your way to being a Python artisan.

Step 3: Verify Your Python Powers

With Python now on your machine, let's ensure that it's awake and ready.

1. **Open a Terminal or Command Prompt:**
   - **Windows:** Search for "Command Prompt" or "PowerShell" and open it.
   - **Mac/Linux:** Use the terminal. It's your command center.

2. **Type the Magic Incantation:**

```
python --version
```

For Python 3:

```
python3 --version
```

If all is well, you should see Python's version number. Now, you're officially a Python conjurer.

Step 4: Setting Pip Free

Pip, the Python package installer, is your lazy genie for getting Python libraries. Let's set it free:

1. **In the Terminal or Command Prompt:**

```
pip --version
```

Or for Python 3:

```
pip3 --version
```

If it responds, you've unleashed your package genie.

Step 5: Celebrate Your Laziness

Congratulations, you've successfully summoned Python to your command! Feel free to indulge in a well-deserved celebration. Your journey into the world of Pythonic laziness has officially begun. Stay tuned for more coding adventures with your trusty Python companion!

Introduction to IDEs: Your Magical Coding Playground

Ahoy, aspiring wizard of the code realm! Now that you've summoned Python to your lair, it's time to unveil the mystical world of Integrated Development Environments (IDEs). Imagine these as your magical playgrounds where coding dreams come to life, and debugging demons are banished with a flick of your programming wand.

Chapter Highlights

- **The Magic of IDEs:** An IDE is not just a tool; it's your secret workshop where the mundane becomes magical. It's like having a personal coding genie at your service.

- **Choosing Your Spellbook:** Just as a wizard selects their favorite spellbook, you get to choose your IDE. We'll explore a few enchanting options, each with its own special powers.

- **Wands, Cauldrons, and Debugging Potions:** Get ready for a whimsical tour of the essential features in your IDE toolkit. From autocomplete wands to debugging potions, we'll cover it all in a way that's as delightful as brewing a magical elixir.

The Enchanting World of IDEs

An Analogy for the Curious Minds

Picture your IDE as a magical forest. Each tool, feature, and shortcut is a magical creature ready to assist you on your coding quest. The autocomplete fairy completes your thoughts, the debugging phoenix rises from the ashes of errors, and the version control elves ensure harmony in your coding kingdom.

Meet the IDE Wizards

1. **PyCharm, the Sorcerer Supreme:** A powerful wizard with a plethora of spells, PyCharm guides you through the realms of Python with ease. It's your seasoned mentor in the coding arts.

2. **VSCode, the Shape-Shifter:** With its vast marketplace of extensions, VSCode adapts to your coding style like a shape-shifting familiar. It's the chameleon of the coding forest.

3. **Jupyter, the Alchemist:** For those who seek the magic of data science, Jupyter is your alchemical laboratory. It turns raw code into beautiful, interactive spells.

Your First Encounter

Imagine this: you open your chosen IDE, and it welcomes you like an old friend. Your code is colored like a palette of magic, errors are highlighted like mischievous imps, and the run button is your portal to witnessing the spell come to life.

Let's Dive In!

In the chapters ahead, we'll explore each facet of your chosen IDE, learning how to cast spells efficiently, debug with finesse, and create magic potions (code snippets) that work like a charm.

So, dear apprentice of the code arts, fasten your robes and prepare your wand (keyboard), for your journey into the enchanting world of IDEs is about to commence. Welcome to the realm where coding becomes an adventure, and your IDE is the trusty map leading you through the magical forests of Python!

Chapter 6: Your First Python Date

Welcome, eager coder, to the enchanting realm of Python! In this chapter, we embark on your first date with Python—a gentle introduction where we'll hold hands with the Hello World tradition and discover the magic of comments, your trusty companions on this coding journey.

The Hello World Charm

In the land of programming, your first date is often a dance with the timeless tradition of Hello World. It's the moment where you and Python exchange pleasantries, setting the stage for a beautiful coding romance.

Writing Your First Love Note

Open your favorite IDE, summon Python to your command, and let's write your first love note:

```
print("Hello, World!")
```

Ah, the simplicity of it! This single line of code is like a rose offered to the Pythonic muse, and when you run it, you'll witness the magic unfold. The words "Hello, World!" will gracefully appear, marking the beginning of your Pythonic adventure.

Conversations with Python: The Art of Comments

Now, imagine that you and Python are engaging in a conversation, not just through code but with notes sprinkled throughout. These notes, known as comments, are your secret language to communicate with future-you and anyone else who gazes upon your code.

The Comment Chronicles

In Python, comments start with the `#` symbol. They don't affect the code's execution; instead, they offer insights, explanations, and witty remarks to anyone reading your code.

```
# This is a comment. Python ignores it, but
humans rejoice.
print("Hello, World!")  # This comment is like
a whisper, meant only for the keen observer
```

Why Comments Are Your Best Friends

1. **Guiding Lights:** Comments serve as guideposts in the Pythonic wilderness, helping you (and others) navigate the code landscape.

2. **Notes to Self:** When you return to your code after a magical hiatus, comments are like breadcrumbs leading you back to your train of thought.

3. **Team Communication:** If you're collaborating with other wizards, comments become the shared language, ensuring everyone is on the same page.

A Date to Remember

Your first date with Python is not just a ritual; it's a moment etched in the code of time. As you print your first "Hello, World!" and dance with comments, you're laying the foundation for a beautiful coding journey.

Examples

Example 1: Hello World

The traditional "Hello World" program is a simple yet powerful way to introduce yourself to a new programming language. In Python, it looks like this:

```python
# Hello World in Python
print("Hello, World!")
```

Explanation:
- `print()` is a built-in function that outputs text to the console.
- `"Hello, World!"` is a string, enclosed in double quotes. Strings are sequences of characters.

Run this script, and you'll see the friendly greeting displayed on your console.

Using Comments
Example 2: Single-line Comment

```python
# This is a single-line comment
print("Comments are helpful!")  # This comment
explains the print statement
```

Explanation:
- Comments after a `#` are treated as single-line comments.
- They are ignored by the Python interpreter.

Example 3: Multi-line Comment

```python
""" This is a multi-line comment.
```

```
It can span multiple lines, making it useful
for detailed explanations.
"""

print("Multi-line comments add clarity.")
```

Explanation:
- Multi-line comments are created using triple-quotes (`"""` or `'''`).
- Everything between the triple-quotes is treated as a comment.

Chapter 7: The Pythonic Way

Ah, dear reader, you've embarked on a journey with Python, and now it's time to not just write code but to dance with it in the Pythonic ballroom. In this chapter, we'll waltz through the principles that make Python a language of elegance, readability, and sheer beauty.

Embracing Pythonic Philosophy

In the Pythonic kingdom, there exists a philosophy—a way of thinking and coding that goes beyond mere syntax. To truly master Python, you must embrace the Pythonic philosophy, where simplicity, clarity, and beauty reign supreme.

The Zen of Python

Behold, the Zen of Python—a poetic manifesto written by Tim Peters that encapsulates the guiding principles of Pythonic thinking. Let's explore a few verses:

```
import this
```

The Zen of Python whispers:

- Beautiful is better than ugly.
- Simple is better than complex.
- Readability counts.

Readability: The Elegance of Clarity

Imagine your code as a piece of literature, meant to be read and understood by both humans and machines. Python values readability as a cornerstone of its philosophy.

The Art of Indentation

In Python, indentation is not just a stylistic choice; it's the language's heartbeat. Proper indentation replaces cumbersome braces, guiding the reader through the code's flow.

```
# Non-Pythonic
if x:
    do_something()
    do_another_thing()

# Pythonic
if x:
    do_something()
    do_another_thing()
```

Meaningful Names

In the Pythonic kingdom, naming conventions are sacred. Choose names that tell a story, not just variables and functions. A well-named variable is a tale waiting to be told.

```
# Non-Pythonic
a = 10   # What is 'a'?

# Pythonic
number_of_students = 10   # Ah, clarity!
```

Simplicity: The Elegance of Efficiency

Simplicity is the essence of Pythonic elegance. While it can be tempting to dazzle with complex code acrobatics, Python encourages a straightforward approach.

List Comprehensions

Witness the beauty of list comprehensions—a concise and readable way to create lists:

```
# Non-Pythonic
squares = []
for x in range(10):
    squares.append(x**2)

# Pythonic
squares = [x**2 for x in range(10)]
```

Beauty: The Elegance of Expression

In Python, code is not just a set of instructions; it's a form of expression. Beautiful code flows like poetry, capturing the essence of the task at hand.

Pythonic Idioms

Discover Pythonic idioms—expressions that embody the spirit of Pythonic beauty:

```
# Non-Pythonic
if x != 0:
    do_something()

# Pythonic
if x:
    do_something()
```

A Symphony of Code

As you waltz through the Pythonic ballroom, remember that your code is a symphony. Each line, each character, is a note in the dance of programming. Embrace the Zen of Python, let readability be your guide, simplicity your dance partner, and beauty your inspiration.

Examples
Embrace the Pythonic Philosophy:

Pythonic code is not just a set of rules; it's a way of thinking and writing code that aligns with Python's design principles. Let's explore the key aspects of Pythonic programming.

Readability Matters:

Example 1: Pythonic Variable Naming

```
# Non-Pythonic
x = 10
y = 20

# Pythonic
width = 10
height = 20
```

Explanation:
- Pythonic code uses descriptive variable names, making it clear and readable.

Example 2: Pythonic List Comprehension

```
# Non-Pythonic
squares = []
for i in range(10):
    squares.append(i**2)

# Pythonic
squares = [i**2 for i in range(10)]
```

Explanation:
- Pythonic code leverages list comprehensions for concise and readable iterations.

Simplicity Leads to Elegance:

Example 3: Pythonic Function Definition

```python
# Non-Pythonic
def add_numbers(x, y):
    result = x + y
    return result

# Pythonic
def add_numbers(x, y):
    return x + y
```

Explanation:
- Pythonic functions are concise, with unnecessary intermediate variables eliminated.

Example 4: Pythonic Way to Check for Membership

```python
# Non-Pythonic
if name in names.keys() and names[name] > 0:
    # do something

# Pythonic
if name in names and names[name] > 0:
    # do something
```

Explanation:
- Pythonic code is direct and avoids unnecessary checks.

Beauty in Code:

Example 5: Pythonic Use of Enumerate

```python
# Non-Pythonic
index = 0
for item in my_list:
    print(index, item)
    index += 1

# Pythonic
for index, item in enumerate(my_list):
    print(index, item)
```

Explanation:
- Pythonic code uses built-in functions like `enumerate` for elegant solutions.

Example 6: Pythonic List Slicing

```python
# Non-Pythonic
sublist = []
for i in range(3, 7):
    sublist.append(my_list[i])

# Pythonic
sublist = my_list[3:7]
```

Explanation:
- Pythonic code utilizes list slicing for compact and readable code.

Chapter 8: Variables - Your Memory in Python

Ah, the dance floor is set, and our Pythonic waltz continues! In this chapter, we'll unravel the enchanting world of variables—your memory keepers in Python. Get ready to understand their role, establish a connection with them, and, true to our lazy philosophy, learn naming conventions that are as effortless as a gentle sway.

The Magic of Variables

In Python, variables are like the dancers in our coding waltz. They hold memories, carry values, and make our programs dynamic and flexible.

Variable Assignment

To give life to a variable, we use the assignment operator (`=`):

```
# Assigning values to variables
age = 25
name = "Pyra"
temperature = 98.6
```

In this dance, `age`, `name`, and `temperature` are now partners, holding specific values.

Dynamic Typing

Python is like a masquerade ball where dancers can change their costumes at will. It's dynamically typed, meaning a variable can switch its type:

```
# Dynamic typing
age = 25       # age is an integer
age = "young" # age is now a string
```

Naming Conventions: The Lazy Way

Ah, naming conventions—a necessary step in our dance. But fear not, for we shall approach this with the elegance of the lazy dancer. Here's a quick guide:

1. Descriptive Laziness

Choose names that tell a story. Lazy, yes, but meaningful:

```
# Non-Lazy
a = 10

# Lazy, yet meaningful
number_of_students = 10
```

2. Snake_case Serenity

In our Pythonic waltz, we follow the serpentine trail with snake_case. Lowercase words, connected by underscores:

```
# Non-Snakey
NumberOfStudents = 10

# Snakey
number_of_students = 10
```

3. Laziness Loves Clarity

Short and sweet, but not cryptic. A lazy programmer values clarity:

```
# Non-Clarity
tnofst = 10

# Clarity in Laziness
num_students = 10
```

Laziness vs. Laziness

The lazy way isn't about shortcuts; it's about efficiency. We strive for names that are easy on the fingers and clear to the eyes. As you waltz through your Pythonic code, let your variables sway with the rhythm of clarity and simplicity.

Examples
Example 1: Basic Variable Assignment

```
# Basic variable assignment
name = "Alice"
age = 25
is_student = True
```

Explanation:
- Variables (`name`, `age`, `is_student`) store different types of data (string, integer, boolean).
- Python automatically infers the data type.

Example 2: Dynamic Typing in Action

```python
# Dynamic typing in Python
variable_1 = 42
print("Variable 1:", variable_1)

variable_1 = "Python"
print("Variable 1 now:", variable_1)
```

Explanation:
- Python is dynamically typed, allowing variables to change their type during runtime.
- This flexibility simplifies code but requires careful consideration.

Example 3: Variable Reassignment

```python
# Variable reassignment
x = 5
print("Initial x:", x)

x = x + 3
print("Updated x:", x)
```

Explanation:
- Variables can be reassigned with new values.
- This flexibility is useful for iterative operations.

Example 4: Lazy Naming

```python
# Non-Lazy
total_items_in_cart = 10
```

```
average_price_of_products = 25.5

# Lazy
total_items = 10
avg_price = 25.5
```

Explanation:
- Lazy naming favors brevity without sacrificing clarity.
- Choose names that convey meaning without unnecessary verbosity.

Example 5: Naming Conventions for Constants

```
# Constants in Python (non-lazy way)
PI = 3.14
GRAVITY = 9.8

# Lazy Constants
pi = 3.14
gravity = 9.8
```

Explanation:
- Constants are typically named using uppercase letters.
- Lazy conventions still follow this, but without shouting.

Simple App: Personal Information Tracker

Let's create a basic console-based application that captures and displays personal information using variables.

```
# Personal Information Tracker App

# Get user input
name = input("Enter your name: ")
age = int(input("Enter your age: "))
city = input("Enter your city: ")

# Display user information
print("\nPersonal Information:")
print("Name:", name)
print("Age:", age)
print("City:", city)
```

Explanation:
- The variables `name`, `age`, and `city` store user input.
- The `print` statements display the stored information.

Chapter 9: Data Types Made Simple

Welcome, dance partner of Pythonic elegance! In this chapter, we'll twirl through the enchanting realm of data types, where integers, floats, and strings perform a harmonious ballet. Prepare to be captivated by the dynamic nature of Python's typing, where variables can change costumes effortlessly.

The Dance of Data Types

In the Pythonic ball, data types are like different dance styles—each with its own rhythm and steps. Let's explore the fundamental types: integers (`int`), floats (`float`), and strings (`str`).

1. Integers - The Waltz of Whole Numbers

Integers are the noble dancers of the whole number waltz. They can be positive or negative, allowing you to count, calculate, and move gracefully through the world of numbers.

```
age = 25
students = -15
```

2. Floats - The Ballet of Decimals

Floats are the agile ballet dancers, capable of gliding through the intricate world of decimals. They add finesse to mathematical operations.

```
temperature = 98.6
pi_value = 3.14
```

3. Strings - The Tango of Text

Strings are the passionate tango dancers, entwining characters in their embrace. They allow you to work with text, creating stories and messages.

```
name = "Pyra"
quote = "Coding is poetry in motion."
```

Dynamic Typing Unveiled

In our Pythonic dance, the magic of dynamic typing shines. Variables can change their type at runtime, like dancers gracefully switching costumes.

```
x = 42      # x is an integer
x = "hello" # x is now a string
```

This dynamic flexibility is what makes Python feel like a masquerade ball, where dancers can change roles effortlessly.

Lazy Dance Partnerships

In our lazy waltz, working with data types is as simple as a two-step. Python is inherently lazy-friendly, handling type conversions behind the scenes:

```
# Lazy addition of an integer and a float
result = 10 + 5.0  # No explicit conversion
needed
```

The Pythonic Harmony

As you dance through the Pythonic ball, let the beauty of data types enrich your code. Whether you're counting, calculating, or telling stories, Python's dynamic typing and expressive data types ensure a symphony of elegance.

Examples
Example 1: Integers (`int`)

```
# Integer data type
```

```
age = 25
```

Explanation:
- Integers represent whole numbers without decimal points.
- In the example, `age` is assigned the integer value of 25.

Example 2: Floating-Point Numbers (`float`)

```
# Float data type
height = 1.75
```

Explanation:
- Floating-point numbers represent real numbers with decimal points.
- `height` is assigned the floating-point value of 1.75.

Example 3: Strings (`str`)

```
# String data type
name = "Alice"
```

Explanation:
- Strings are sequences of characters enclosed in quotes.
- `name` is assigned the string value "Alice".

Example 4: Dynamic Typing

```
# Dynamic typing in Python
variable_1 = 42
print("Variable 1:", variable_1)
```

```python
variable_1 = "Python"
print("Variable 1 now:", variable_1)
```

Explanation:
- Python is dynamically typed, allowing variables to change type during runtime.
- `variable_1` initially holds an integer and later becomes a string.

Simple App: Calculator

Let's create a basic console-based calculator application that showcases the use of different data types.

```python
# Calculator App

# Get user input
num1 = float(input("Enter the first number: "))
num2 = float(input("Enter the second number: "))

# Perform calculations
sum_result = num1 + num2
difference_result = num1 - num2
product_result = num1 * num2
quotient_result = num1 / num2

# Display results
print("\nCalculator Results:")
print("Sum:", sum_result)
print("Difference:", difference_result)
```

```
print("Product:", product_result)
print("Quotient:", quotient_result)
```

Explanation:
- User inputs are converted to floating-point numbers (`float`) to allow decimal inputs.
- Calculations are performed using various operators (`+`, `-`, `*`, `/`).
- Results are displayed using the `print` statements.

Chapter 10: Playing with Lists and Tuples

Ah, welcome back to our Pythonic ballroom, dear dancer of code! In this chapter, we'll pirouette through the world of lists and tuples—your steadfast dance partners when it comes to organizing and manipulating data. Get ready for a lively performance, where list comprehensions will dazzle you with their elegance and simplicity.

Lists: The Dance of Flexibility

In our Pythonic ball, lists are like a dance floor where elements move freely, creating a dynamic and expressive performance.

Creating Lists

```
# Creating a list of numbers
ages = [25, 30, 22, 40]

# A list of names
```

```
names = ["Alice", "Bob", "Charlie"]
```

Accessing and Slicing

Just like skilled dancers, lists allow you to access and slice with finesse:

```
# Accessing elements
print(ages[0])   # Output: 25

# Slicing
print(names[1:])   # Output: ["Bob", "Charlie"]
```

Modifying and Adding Moves

In our dynamic dance, you can modify and add new elements effortlessly:

```
# Modifying an element
ages[1] = 31

# Adding a new element
names.append("David")
```

Tuples: The Graceful Ballet

Tuples are the graceful ballet dancers—immutable, ordered, and elegant in their simplicity.

Creating Tuples

```
# Creating a tuple of coordinates
point = (3, 7)

# A tuple of colors
rgb = (255, 0, 0)
```

Unpacking Elegance

Unpacking allows you to gracefully assign values from a tuple:

```
# Unpacking coordinates
x, y = point
```

List Comprehensions: The Choreography of Elegance

List comprehensions are the choreography of elegance—a concise way to create lists. Let's marvel at their beauty:

```
# Creating a list of squares using a loop
squares = []
for x in range(5):
    squares.append(x**2)

# The Pythonic way with a list comprehension
squares = [x**2 for x in range(5)]
```

List comprehensions encapsulate the essence of Pythonic beauty, making your code concise and expressive.

Lazy Dancer's Guide

In our lazy waltz, lists and tuples are your trusty partners. With their flexibility and simplicity, you can elegantly organize and manipulate data. List comprehensions, like a well-choreographed routine, add a touch of flair to your Pythonic dance.

Examples
Example 1: Lists

```python
# Creating a list
fruits = ["apple", "banana", "orange", "grape"]

# Accessing elements
first_fruit = fruits[0]
last_fruit = fruits[-1]

# Modifying elements
fruits[1] = "kiwi"

# Adding elements
fruits.append("mango")

# Removing elements
removed_fruit = fruits.pop(2)
```

Explanation:
- Lists are ordered collections that can contain elements of different data types.
- Indexing starts at 0, and negative indices count from the end.
- Lists are mutable; you can modify, add, and remove elements.

Example 2: Tuples

```python
# Creating a tuple
coordinates = (10, 20)

# Accessing elements
x = coordinates[0]
y = coordinates[1]
```

Explanation:
- Tuples are ordered collections similar to lists but are immutable.
- Once a tuple is created, you cannot modify its elements.

Example 3: List Comprehension

```python
# List comprehension to create a list of
squares
squares = [x**2 for x in range(5)]

# List comprehension with condition
even_squares = [x**2 for x in range(10) if x %
2 == 0]
```

Explanation:
- List comprehensions provide a concise way to create lists.
- They consist of an expression followed by a `for` loop (and an optional `if` condition).

Simple App: Task Manager

Let's create a basic console-based task manager application using lists.

```python
# Task Manager App

# Initialize an empty task list
tasks = []

# Add tasks to the list
tasks.append("Complete chapter 10")
tasks.append("Submit work to editor")
tasks.append("Celebrate progress")

# Display tasks using list comprehension
print("\nTasks for Today:")
[print(f"{index + 1}. {task}") for index, task
in enumerate(tasks)]
```

Explanation:
- The `tasks` list stores the user's tasks.
- List comprehension is used to display tasks with their index.

Chapter 11: Dictionaries - Your Pythonic Notepad

Welcome, dear dancer of code, to the Pythonic ballroom where dictionaries take the stage. In this chapter, we'll unravel the magic of dictionaries—a versatile partner that transforms the dance floor into a notepad for storing and retrieving information. Get ready to explore real-world applications and master the lazy art of dictionary manipulation.

Dictionaries: The Notepad of Python

In the dance of data structures, dictionaries are like a notepad, allowing you to jot down information in key-value pairs. Let's begin with the basics:

```python
# Creating a dictionary of person information
person = {
    "name": "Alice",
    "age": 30,
    "occupation": "Engineer"
}
```

Here, "name," "age," and "occupation" are keys, and "Alice," 30, and "Engineer" are their corresponding values.

Real-World Applications: The Dance of Information

Dictionaries shine in real-world scenarios, acting as notepads for varied information. Consider a contacts book:

```python
# Contacts book
contacts = {
    "Alice": "alice@email.com",
    "Bob": "bob@email.com",
    "Charlie": "charlie@email.com"
}
```

In this dance, names are keys, and emails are values. Retrieving Charlie's email is as simple as:

```python
charlies_email = contacts["Charlie"]
```

Lazy Guide to Dictionary Manipulation

In our Pythonic waltz, manipulating dictionaries is a lazy affair with these elegant moves:

Adding a New Entry

```
# Adding a new contact
contacts["David"] = "david@email.com"
```

Modifying an Entry

```
# Modifying Bob's email
contacts["Bob"] = "bob.new@email.com"
```

Checking if a Key Exists

```
# Checking if Alice is in contacts
if "Alice" in contacts:
    print("Alice is in the contacts book!")
```

Removing an Entry

```
# Removing Charlie from contacts
del contacts["Charlie"]
```

Lazy Beauty in Dictionary Comprehensions

Just as list comprehensions added elegance to our routine, dictionary comprehensions bring lazy beauty to dictionary creation:

```
# Creating a dictionary of squares
squares = {x: x**2 for x in range(5)}
```

Lazy Dancer's Guide

Dictionaries are your Pythonic notepad, offering a versatile way to store and retrieve information. Real-world applications, lazy manipulation techniques, and the elegance of comprehensions make dictionaries an essential partner in your Pythonic dance.

Examples
Example 1: Creating a Dictionary

```
# Creating a dictionary to store information
about a person
person = {
    "name": "Alice",
    "age": 30,
    "city": "Wonderland"
}
```

Explanation:
- Dictionaries are unordered collections of key-value pairs.
- Each key must be unique and is associated with a value.
- In this example, the dictionary stores information about a person.

Example 2: Accessing and Modifying Dictionary Elements

```python
# Accessing elements
person_name = person["name"]
person_age = person.get("age", "N/A")

# Modifying elements
person["city"] = "New Wonderland"
person["gender"] = "Female"
```

Explanation:
- You can access values using their keys.
- The `get` method is used to access a key with a default value if the key is not found.
- Dictionary values can be modified or new key-value pairs added.

Example 3: Lazy Dictionary Initialization

```python
# Lazy initialization of a dictionary
lazy_dict = {}

# Lazy addition of key-value pairs
lazy_dict["lazy_level"] = "Expert"
lazy_dict.setdefault("pythonista", True)
```

Explanation:
- Dictionaries can be lazily initialized and populated.
- The `setdefault` method sets a default value if the key is not already in the dictionary.

Example 4: Dictionary Comprehension

```
# Dictionary comprehension to create a
dictionary of squares
squares_dict = {x: x**2 for x in range(5)}
```

Explanation:
- Similar to list comprehensions, dictionary comprehensions
provide a concise way to create dictionaries.

Simple App: Contact Manager

Let's create a basic console-based contact manager application
using dictionaries.

```
# Contact Manager App

# Initialize an empty contact dictionary
contacts = {}

# Add contacts
contacts["Alice"] = {"phone": "123-456-7890",
"email": "alice@email.com"}
contacts["Bob"] = {"phone": "987-654-3210",
"email": "bob@email.com"}

# Display contact information
print("\nContact Information:")
for name, info in contacts.items():
    print(f"\n{name}'s Details:")
    print("Phone:", info["phone"])
    print("Email:", info["email"])
```

Explanation:
- The `contacts` dictionary stores contact information.
- The application displays contact details using a loop through the dictionary items.

Chapter 12: Control Flow - Taking Charge

Welcome, adept dancer of code, to the crescendo of our Pythonic waltz! In this chapter, we take charge of our dance floor with the artful mastery of control flow. Prepare to make decisions with lazy elegance using if statements and effortlessly loop through the beats of your code with loops.

If Statements: Decisions for the Lazy Mind

In the dance of programming, if statements are your partners for making decisions with grace and simplicity. Let's explore:

The Lazy Decision

```
# Making a decision with an if statement
age = 25

if age < 30:
    print("Young and vibrant!")
else:
    print("Experienced and wise!")
```

Here, the lazy mind makes a decision based on age—simple and effective.

The Ternary Elegance

For the minimalist dancer, the ternary operator offers a concise way to make decisions:

```
# Ternary elegance
message = "Young and vibrant!" if age < 30 else
"Experienced and wise!"
print(message)
```

Loops: Doing More with Less Effort

In our Pythonic dance, loops are like the repetitive yet graceful steps that allow us to traverse data with ease.

The Lazy Loop

```
# The lazy loop: printing numbers from 1 to 5
for number in range(1, 6):
    print(number)
```

Lazy minds adore the simplicity of a loop, effortlessly printing numbers in a range.

The Elegance of List Comprehensions in Loops

Combine the power of loops with the elegance of list comprehensions:

```
# Using a list comprehension in a loop
squares = [x**2 for x in range(1, 6)]
```

```
print(squares)
```

Lazy Dancer's Guide to Control Flow

In our grand finale, take charge of your Pythonic dance floor with these lazy moves:

Breaking Out of the Loop

```
# Breaking out of the loop when a condition is
met
for number in range(1, 11):
    if number == 5:
        break
    print(number)
```

Skipping to the Next Iteration

```
# Skipping to the next iteration when a
condition is met
for number in range(1, 11):
    if number % 2 == 0:
        continue
    print(number)
```

The Grand Finale

As we conclude our Pythonic waltz through control flow, you've now mastered the art of making decisions and effortlessly looping through the beats of your code. Your Pythonic dance is now a symphony of elegance and lazy efficiency.

Example 1: Simple If Statement

```
# Simple if statement
age = 25

if age < 30:
    print("You're still in your prime!")
```

Explanation:
- If statements allow you to make decisions based on conditions.
- The code inside the indented block (after `if`) runs only if the condition is true.

Example 2: If-Else Statement

```
# If-else statement
temperature = 28

if temperature > 30:
    print("It's a hot day!")
else:
    print("Enjoy the weather!")
```

Explanation:
- If the condition after `if` is false, the code in the `else` block executes.

Example 3: Nested If Statements

```python
# Nested if statements
age = 18
is_student = True

if age < 25:
    if is_student:
        print("You qualify for a student
discount!")
    else:
        print("Enjoy the regular discount.")
else:
    print("Sorry, no discounts for you.")
```

Explanation:
- You can nest if statements to create more complex decision structures.

Example 4: While Loop

```python
# While loop to print numbers from 1 to 5
count = 1

while count <= 5:
    print(count)
    count += 1
```

Explanation:
- While loops continue to execute as long as the condition is true.

Example 5: For Loop

```python
# For loop to iterate over a list
fruits = ["apple", "banana", "orange"]

for fruit in fruits:
    print(fruit)
```

Explanation:
- For loops, iterate over a sequence (e.g., a list) and execute the block of code for each element.

Simple App: Task Scheduler

Let's create a basic console-based task scheduler application using control flow.

```python
# Task Scheduler App

# List of tasks
tasks = ["Write Chapter 12", "Submit Work",
"Take a Break"]

# Print tasks using a for loop
print("\nTasks for Today:")
for task in tasks:
    print(task)

# Check if tasks are completed
for task in tasks:
    if input(f"Did you complete '{task}'?
(yes/no): ").lower() == "yes":
        print(f"Congratulations on completing
```

```
'{task}'!")
    else:
        print(f"Don't forget to complete
'{task}'!")
```

Explanation:
- The application uses a combination of for loops and if statements to manage and check completion of tasks.

Chapter 13: Functions - Your Python Helpers

Dear conductor of the Pythonic symphony, in this chapter, we explore the harmonious world of functions—a magnificent ensemble of reusable code. You will learn to define and call functions, and discover the power of default arguments, the lazy programmer's best friend.

Functions: The Virtuoso Performers

In our Pythonic orchestra, functions are the virtuoso performers, each playing a unique role in the composition of your code.

Defining Functions

```
# Defining a simple function
def greet(name):
    return f"Hello, {name}!"
```

With this function, you've composed a musical note—a greeting that can be played for anyone.

Calling Functions

```python
# Calling the greet function
message = greet("Alice")
print(message)
```

The lazy conductor directs the musicians, and with a call, the function performs its melody.

Default Arguments: The Lazy Programmer's Best Friend

Default arguments are like a preset melody in our musical score, ready to play unless directed otherwise.

Lazy Greetings

```python
# Adding a default argument
def greet(name="stranger"):
    return f"Hello, {name}!"
```

Now, even if you don't specify a name, the function plays a tune for "stranger."

```python
message = greet()
print(message)  # Output: "Hello, stranger!"
```

Lazy Dancer's Guide to Functions

In our Pythonic symphony, functions are your virtuoso helpers, bringing order and reusability to your code. Embrace these lazy moves:

Returning Multiple Values

```python
# Returning multiple values from a function
def get_name_and_age():
    name = "Alice"
    age = 30
    return name, age

# Unpacking the values
name, age = get_name_and_age()
```

Lambda Functions: The Mini Maestros

```python
# Creating a lambda function
double = lambda x: x * 2
result = double(5)  # Result: 10
```

The Overture to Advanced Python

As we conclude our exploration of functions, you've unlocked the power to create reusable code and leverage default arguments for lazy efficiency. The Pythonic symphony continues, and in our final chapter, we'll embark on the overture to advanced Python, revealing the secrets of modules, packages, and the grandeur of Pythonic libraries. Prepare for the crescendo, where you become the master composer of Pythonic melodies!

Examples
Example 1: Simple Function

```
# Defining a simple function
def greet(name):
    print(f"Hello, {name}!")

# Calling the function
greet("Alice")
```

Explanation:
- Functions are defined using the `def` keyword.
- The function name is followed by parentheses containing parameters.
- Code inside the function is indented and executed when the function is called.

Example 2: Function with Return Value

```
# Function with a return value
def add_numbers(x, y):
    return x + y

# Calling the function and storing the result
result = add_numbers(3, 5)
print("Sum:", result)
```

Explanation:
- Functions can return values using the `return` keyword.
- The returned value can be stored in a variable or used directly.

Example 3: Function with Default Argument

```
# Function with default argument
```

```
def greet_lazy(name, greeting="Hello"):
    print(f"{greeting}, {name}!")

# Calling the function without providing the
'greeting' argument
greet_lazy("Bob")
```

Explanation:
- Default arguments have a default value if not provided during the function call.
- This allows for flexibility while keeping the code concise.

Example 4: Function with Multiple Default Arguments

```
# Function with multiple default arguments
def make_smoothie(fruit="banana",
liquid="milk", ice=True):
    print(f"Making a smoothie with {fruit},
{liquid}, and {'ice' if ice else 'no ice'}.")

# Calling the function with different
combinations of arguments
make_smoothie()
make_smoothie("strawberry", "yogurt")
```

Explanation:
- Functions can have multiple default arguments.
- You can override the defaults by providing values during the function call.

Simple App: Lazy Calculator

Let's create a basic console-based calculator application using functions.

```python
# Lazy Calculator App

# Function to add two numbers with a default
value for the second number
def add_numbers(x, y=0):
    return x + y

# Function to subtract two numbers
def subtract_numbers(x, y):
    return x - y

# Function to multiply two numbers with a
default value for the second number
def multiply_numbers(x, y=1):
    return x * y

# Function to divide two numbers
def divide_numbers(x, y):
    if y != 0:
        return x / y
    else:
        return "Cannot divide by zero."

# Using the functions
print("Sum:", add_numbers(5))
print("Difference:", subtract_numbers(8, 3))
print("Product:", multiply_numbers(4))
```

```
print("Quotient:", divide_numbers(10, 2))
```

Explanation:
- The calculator application uses functions for basic arithmetic operations.
- Default values for some parameters make the functions more flexible.

Chapter 14: Modules and Libraries - Borrowing Code

Dear composer of Pythonic melodies, in this chapter, we unravel the art of borrowing code—importing modules seamlessly and exploring commonly used libraries. Get ready to enhance your Pythonic symphony with the grandeur of modules and the richness of libraries.

Importing Modules: The Gentle Borrowing

In our Pythonic orchestra, modules are the sections, each bringing a unique set of instruments to enrich our musical composition.

Simple Import

```
# Importing the math module
import math

# Using a function from the math module
result = math.sqrt(25)
```

The lazy conductor simply says, "Bring in the math instruments," and the orchestra plays a delightful square root.

Aliasing for Laziness

```
# Aliasing a module for brevity
import pandas as pd
data = pd.read_csv("data.csv")
```

Now, the pandas library answers to the concise call of "pd."

Introduction to Commonly Used Libraries

In the vast library of Pythonic compositions, certain libraries stand out as commonly used maestros, ready to elevate your symphony.

NumPy: The Virtuoso of Numerical Computing

```
# Using NumPy for numerical operations
import numpy as np
array = np.array([1, 2, 3, 4, 5])
sum_result = np.sum(array)
```

NumPy's powerful instruments transform numerical operations into a musical delight.

Requests: The Magician of Web Requests

```
# Using the Requests library for web requests
import requests
```

```
response =
requests.get("https://www.example.com")
```

With Requests, you effortlessly summon web content to enrich
your Pythonic score.

Matplotlib: The Visual Composer

```
# Using Matplotlib for visualizations
import matplotlib.pyplot as plt
x = [1, 2, 3, 4, 5]
y = [10, 20, 15, 25, 30]
plt.plot(x, y)
plt.show()
```

Matplotlib orchestrates stunning visualizations, turning data into a
visual symphony.

The Lazy Composer's Guide

In our Pythonic symphony, modules and libraries are the borrowed
notes and instruments that enrich your composition. Embrace these
lazy moves:

Selective Imports

```
# Selective imports for precision
from math import sqrt
result = sqrt(25)
```

Exploring Library Documentation

```
# Seeking guidance in documentation
import pandas as pd
help(pd)
```

The Grandeur of Pythonic Libraries

As we conclude our exploration of modules and libraries, you've learned to borrow code with elegance and integrate the grandeur of commonly used Pythonic maestros. The symphony continues, and in the final chapter, we embark on a journey through the Pythonic landscape, unveiling tips, best practices, and the art of becoming a Pythonic virtuoso. Prepare for the crescendo, where you take the stage as the master composer of Pythonic melodies!

Examples
Example 1: Basic Module Import

```
# Importing the 'math' module
import math

# Using functions from the 'math' module
radius = 5
area = math.pi * math.pow(radius, 2)
print(f"The area of a circle with radius
{radius} is {area:.2f}.")
```

Explanation:
- Modules contain reusable code and can be imported using the `import` keyword.

- The `math` module provides mathematical functions and constants.

Example 2: Module Alias

```python
# Importing the 'random' module with an alias
import random as rnd

# Using functions from the 'random' module with
the alias
random_number = rnd.randint(1, 10)
print(f"Random number: {random_number}")
```

Explanation:
- You can use an alias to shorten the module name during import.

Example 3: Using the `datetime` Library

```python
# Using the 'datetime' library
from datetime import datetime

# Getting the current date and time
current_datetime = datetime.now()
print(f"Current date and time:
{current_datetime}")
```

Explanation:
- The `datetime` library provides functionalities for working with dates and times.
- The `datetime.now()` function returns the current date and time.

Example 4: Using the `requests` Library

```python
# Using the 'requests' library to fetch data
from a URL
import requests

# Fetching data from a URL
response =
requests.get("https://www.example.com")
print(f"Status code: {response.status_code}")
```

Explanation:
- The `requests` library simplifies making HTTP requests.

Simple App: Lazy Weather Checker

Let's create a basic console-based weather checker application using a library.

```python
# Lazy Weather Checker App

# Using the 'requests' library to fetch weather
data
import requests

def get_weather(city):
    # Replace 'your_api_key' with a valid API
key from an open weather API
    api_key = 'your_api_key'
    url =
f"http://api.openweathermap.org/data/2.5/weathe
```

```
r?q={city}&appid={api_key}"

    response = requests.get(url)
    weather_data = response.json()

    temperature = weather_data['main']['temp']
    description =
weather_data['weather'][0]['description']

    return temperature, description

# Get user input
city_name = input("Enter the name of your city:
")

# Get and display weather information
temperature, description =
get_weather(city_name)
print(f"\nCurrent weather in {city_name}:")
print(f"Temperature: {temperature}°C")
print(f"Description: {description}")
```

Explanation:
- The application uses the `requests` library to fetch weather data from an API.
- The API key needs to be replaced with a valid key from an open weather API.

Chapter 15: File Handling - Lazy Persistence

Dear Pythonic virtuoso, in this chapter, we explore the art of lazy persistence—reading and writing files with ease. Get ready to orchestrate your data with the lazy grace of file handling, making CSV and JSON interactions a seamless part of your Pythonic symphony.

Reading Files: A Melodic Prelude

In our Pythonic symphony, reading files is akin to opening a musical score, revealing the notes stored within.

Reading Text Files

```
# Reading a text file
file_path = "sample.txt"

with open(file_path, "r") as file:
    content = file.read()

print(content)
```

The lazy conductor merely opens the score and lets Python read the notes, encapsulated in the "with" statement for automatic file closure.

Writing Files: A Serenade to Persistence

To compose your own notes, writing files is the key, adding your melodies to the grand symphony.

Writing to Text Files

```
# Writing to a text file
```

```
output_path = "output.txt"
melody = "This is my Pythonic composition."

with open(output_path, "w") as file:
    file.write(melody)
```

With the gentle stroke of the file.write() bow, your melody is
inscribed on the musical scroll.

CSV and JSON: Lazy Formats for Lazy Programmers

CSV and JSON are the lazy programmer's best friends for storing
structured data.

CSV: The Lazy Spreadsheet

```
import csv

# Writing to a CSV file
csv_path = "data.csv"
data = [["Alice", 25], ["Bob", 30], ["Charlie",
22]]

with open(csv_path, "w", newline="") as file:
    writer = csv.writer(file)
    writer.writerows(data)
```

The CSV maestro, csv.writer(), arranges your data in rows and
columns with lazy elegance.

JSON: The Lazy Dictionary

```python
import json

# Writing to a JSON file
json_path = "data.json"
data_dict = {"Alice": 25, "Bob": 30, "Charlie":
22}

with open(json_path, "w") as file:
    json.dump(data_dict, file)
```

JSON.dump() transforms your dictionary into a lazy JSON
structure—a harmonious arrangement for lazy programmers.

The Lazy Composer's Guide

In our grand finale, file handling becomes the encore, allowing
your Pythonic symphony to persist beyond the ephemeral runtime.
Embrace these lazy moves:

Handling File Paths

```python
import os

# Handling file paths lazily
file_name = "data.txt"
file_path = os.path.join("folder", file_name)
```

The os.path.join() harmony constructs file paths with lazy ease.

Lazy Reading Line by Line

```
# Lazy reading line by line
file_path = "sample.txt"

with open(file_path, "r") as file:
    for line in file:
        print(line)
```

This lazy loop reads a file line by line, allowing Python to dance through the notes.

Examples
Example 1: Writing to a Text File

```
# Writing to a text file
with open('sample.txt', 'w') as file:
    file.write("Hello, lazy programmers!\n")
    file.write("Welcome to the world of file
handling.")
```

Explanation:
- The `open` function is used to open a file.
- The `'w'` parameter specifies that the file is opened for writing.
- The `with` statement ensures that the file is properly closed after writing.

Example 2: Reading from a Text File

```
# Reading from a text file
with open('sample.txt', 'r') as file:
```

```
    content = file.read()
    print(content)
```

Explanation:
- The `r` parameter in the `open` function specifies that the file is opened for reading.
- The `read` method reads the entire content of the file.

Example 3: Writing to a CSV File

```
# Writing to a CSV file
import csv

data = [['Name', 'Age', 'City'],
        ['Alice', 25, 'Wonderland'],
        ['Bob', 30, 'Lazytown']]

with open('data.csv', 'w', newline='') as
csvfile:
    csv_writer = csv.writer(csvfile)
    csv_writer.writerows(data)
```

Explanation:
- The `csv` module simplifies working with CSV files.
- The `newline=''` parameter is important for cross-platform compatibility.

Example 4: Reading from a CSV File

```
# Reading from a CSV file
```

```python
with open('data.csv', 'r') as csvfile:
    csv_reader = csv.reader(csvfile)
    for row in csv_reader:
        print(row)
```

Explanation:
- The `csv.reader` object is used to read the contents of the CSV file row by row.

Example 5: Writing to a JSON File

```python
# Writing to a JSON file
import json

data = {
    'name': 'Alice',
    'age': 25,
    'city': 'Wonderland'
}

with open('data.json', 'w') as jsonfile:
    json.dump(data, jsonfile, indent=2)
```

Explanation:
- The `json` module simplifies working with JSON files.
- The `indent` parameter in `json.dump` adds indentation for better readability.

Example 6: Reading from a JSON File

```python
# Reading from a JSON file
with open('data.json', 'r') as jsonfile:
    loaded_data = json.load(jsonfile)
    print(loaded_data)
```

Explanation:
- The `json.load` method is used to load data from a JSON file.

Simple App: Lazy ToDo List

Let's create a basic console-based ToDo list application using file handling.

```python
# Lazy ToDo List App

# Function to display the ToDo list
def display_todo_list():
    with open('todo.txt', 'r') as file:
        todo_list = file.read()
        print("Your ToDo List:")
        print(todo_list)

# Function to add a task to the ToDo list
def add_to_todo_list(task):
    with open('todo.txt', 'a') as file:
        file.write(f"{task}\n")

# Get user input
task_to_add = input("Enter a task to add to
your ToDo list: ")
```

```
# Add the task to the ToDo list
add_to_todo_list(task_to_add)

# Display the updated ToDo list
display_todo_list()
```

Explanation:
- The ToDo list application uses file handling to read and write tasks to a text file.

Chapter 16: Object-Oriented Laziness

Dear maestro of Pythonic melodies, in this chapter, we step into the realm of object-oriented programming—a harmonious paradigm that allows you to compose code with elegance and efficiency. You'll be introduced to classes and objects, and discover the lazy joy of inheritance.

Classes and Objects: The Symphony of Structure

In the grand composition of Pythonic code, classes are the conductors, orchestrating the harmony of data and functionality. Let's begin our exploration:

Defining a Class

```
# Defining a simple class
class Musician:
    def __init__(self, name, instrument):
        self.name = name
        self.instrument = instrument
```

```python
    def play(self):
        return f"{self.name} plays
{self.instrument}."
```

Here, the `Musician` class is born, with a conductor (`__init__`) and a musician's skill (`play`).

Creating Objects

```python
# Creating objects from the class
guitarist = Musician("Alice", "guitar")
pianist = Musician("Bob", "piano")
```

The lazy composer has crafted two musicians—Alice the guitarist and Bob the pianist.

Inheritance: Laziness Elevated

In the lazy composer's symphony, why write more code when you can inherit it? Inheritance allows you to reuse and extend the functionality of existing classes.

Creating a Subclass

```python
# Creating a subclass
class Drummer(Musician):
    def __init__(self, name):
        super().__init__(name,
instrument="drums")
```

```
    def drum_solo(self):
        return f"{self.name} performs a drum
solo."
```

The `Drummer` class inherits the skills of a `Musician` and adds a special move—a drum solo.

Creating Subclass Objects

```
# Creating objects from the subclass
ringo = Drummer("Ringo")
```

The lazy conductor introduces Ringo, the drummer, inheriting the lazy elegance of the `Musician` class.

Lazy Dancer's Guide to Object-Oriented Laziness

In the grand finale, embrace these lazy moves for object-oriented programming:

Encapsulation: The Art of Hiding

```
# Encapsulation in action
class BankAccount:
    def __init__(self, balance):
        self._balance = balance

    def get_balance(self):
        return self._balance
```

```
def deposit(self, amount):
    self._balance += amount

def withdraw(self, amount):
    if amount <= self._balance:
        self._balance -= amount
    else:
        print("Insufficient funds.")
```

With encapsulation, the lazy composer hides the complexities, revealing only what's necessary.

Polymorphism: The Lazy Harmony

```
# Polymorphism in action
musicians = [guitarist, pianist, ringo]

for musician in musicians:
    print(musician.play())
```

The lazy conductor orchestrates a symphony with diverse musicians, each playing their instrument.

The Pythonic Symphony Elevates

As we conclude our exploration of object-oriented laziness, you've embraced the power of classes, objects, and inheritance. Your Pythonic symphony now resonates with structure, reusability, and the artful harmony of object-oriented principles.

The Pythonic symphony, however, is never truly over. As you continue your journey, may you compose melodies that captivate, inspire, and reflect the lazy elegance of Pythonic programming. Bravo, Pythonic maestro, and may your code dance through the digital realm with everlasting grace!

Examples
Example 1: Creating a Simple Class

```python
# Creating a simple class
class Dog:
    def __init__(self, name, age):
        self.name = name
        self.age = age

    def bark(self):
        print(f"{self.name} says Woof!")

# Creating an object of the class
my_dog = Dog("Buddy", 3)

# Accessing attributes and calling methods
print(f"My dog's name is {my_dog.name} and age is {my_dog.age} years.")
my_dog.bark()
```

Explanation:
- A class is a blueprint for creating objects.
- The `__init__` method is called the constructor and is used to initialize attributes.
- Attributes (like `name` and `age`) store information about the object.

- Methods (like `bark`) represent the behavior of the object.

Example 2: Creating a Subclass

```python
# Creating a subclass using inheritance
class GoldenRetriever(Dog):
    def fetch(self):
        print(f"{self.name} is fetching the
ball!")

# Creating an object of the subclass
golden_dog = GoldenRetriever("Max", 2)

# Accessing attributes and methods from the
parent class and the subclass
print(f"My golden retriever's name is
{golden_dog.name} and age is {golden_dog.age}
years.")
golden_dog.bark()
golden_dog.fetch()
```

Explanation:
- Inheritance allows a new class (subclass) to inherit attributes and methods from an existing class (parent class).
- The `GoldenRetriever` class inherits from the `Dog` class.
- The `fetch` method is specific to the `GoldenRetriever` subclass.

Simple App: Lazy Pet Adoption

Let's create a basic console-based pet adoption application using object-oriented programming.

```python
# Lazy Pet Adoption App

# Base class representing a pet
class Pet:
    def __init__(self, name, age):
        self.name = name
        self.age = age

    def make_sound(self):
        pass  # Placeholder method

# Subclass representing a specific type of pet
class Cat(Pet):
    def make_sound(self):
        print(f"{self.name} says Meow!")

# Subclass representing another type of pet
class Dog(Pet):
    def make_sound(self):
        print(f"{self.name} says Woof!")

# Function to display pet information
def display_pet_info(pet):
    print(f"{pet.name} - {pet.age} years old")
    pet.make_sound()
    print()

# Creating objects of different pet types
my_cat = Cat("Whiskers", 5)
my_dog = Dog("Buddy", 3)
```

```
# Displaying pet information
display_pet_info(my_cat)
display_pet_info(my_dog)
```

Explanation:
- The `Pet` class is a base class representing generic pet attributes and behavior.
- The `Cat` and `Dog` classes are subclasses that inherit from the `Pet` class and provide specific implementations for the `make_sound` method.
- The `display_pet_info` function can work with any pet object, showcasing the flexibility of object-oriented programming.

Chapter 17: Exceptional Laziness

Dear maestro of Pythonic melodies, in this chapter, we dive into the realm of exceptional laziness—handling errors with grace and ease. You'll be introduced to the powerful trio of `try`, `except`, and `finally`, ensuring that your Pythonic symphony remains uninterrupted even in the face of unexpected events.

Handling Errors: The Art of Grace

In the grand composition of Pythonic code, errors are like unexpected dissonances—unwanted but inevitable. Exception handling allows you to navigate through these challenges with grace.

The `try` and `except` Duet

```
# Handling a specific exception
```

```
try:
    result = 10 / 0
except ZeroDivisionError:
    print("Cannot divide by zero.")
```

Here, the lazy conductor attempts a risky move (`10 / 0`), but if it fails, the exception handler gracefully takes over.

The Lazy Error Orchestra

```
# Handling multiple exceptions
try:
    value = int("abc")
except ValueError:
    print("Invalid conversion to int.")
except Exception as e:
    print(f"An unexpected error occurred: {e}")
```

In this symphony, if a ValueError arises, the lazy conductor acknowledges it. For any other unexpected errors, a generic exception handler steps in.

The Trio of `try`, `except`, and `finally`

The `try`, `except`, and `finally` trio is the backbone of lazy error-handling, ensuring that your symphony remains harmonious, even in the face of errors.

The Harmonious Trio

```
# The try, except, and finally trio
try:
    file = open("my_file.txt", "r")
    content = file.read()
except FileNotFoundError:
    print("File not found.")
finally:
    if file:
        file.close()
```

Here, the lazy conductor attempts to open a file, gracefully handles a `FileNotFoundError` if it occurs, and ensures that the file is closed, even in the event of an error.

Lazy Dancer's Guide to Exceptional Laziness

In our grand finale, embrace these lazy moves for exceptional laziness:

Custom Exceptions: The Personalized Choreography

```
# Creating a custom exception
class MelodyError(Exception):
    pass

# Using the custom exception
try:
    raise MelodyError("Something went wrong in the melody.")
except MelodyError as e:
    print(f"MelodyError: {e}")
```

With a custom exception, the lazy conductor personalizes the error choreography, adding a touch of elegance to unexpected events.

The Pythonic Symphony Remains Unbroken

As we conclude our exploration of exceptional laziness, you've learned to handle errors with grace and elegance using the trio of `try`, `except`, and `finally`. Your Pythonic symphony now navigates through the complexities of code with the ease and poise of a seasoned conductor.

The Pythonic symphony, however, is never truly over. As you continue your journey, may you compose melodies that gracefully handle unexpected events, ensuring that your code dances through the digital realm with unwavering elegance. Bravo, Pythonic maestro, and may your symphony play on!

Examples
Example 1: Basic Exception Handling

```
# Basic exception handling
try:
    x = 10 / 0
except ZeroDivisionError as e:
    print(f"Error: {e}")
```

Explanation:
- The `try` block contains the code that might raise an exception.
- The `except` block is executed if an exception of the specified type occurs.

- In this example, a `ZeroDivisionError` is caught, and an error message is printed.

Example 2: Handling Multiple Exceptions

```python
# Handling multiple exceptions
try:
    value = int("hello")
except ValueError:
    print("Invalid conversion to integer.")
except Exception as e:
    print(f"An unexpected error occurred: {e}")
```

Explanation:
- You can have multiple `except` blocks to handle different types of exceptions.
- The first matching `except` block is executed.

Try, Except, Finally: The Lazy Error-Handling Trio

Example 3: Using the `finally` Block

```python
# Using the 'finally' block
try:
    file = open("example.txt", "r")
    content = file.read()
    print(content)
except FileNotFoundError:
    print("File not found.")
finally:
    if file:
```

```
      file.close()
```

Explanation:
- The `finally` block contains code that will be executed no matter what, whether an exception occurs or not.
- In this example, the file is closed in the `finally` block to ensure proper cleanup.

Simple App: Lazy Calculator with Error Handling

Let's enhance our lazy calculator application from Chapter 13 with error handling.

```
# Enhanced Lazy Calculator App with Error
Handling

def divide_numbers(x, y):
    try:
        result = x / y
        return result
    except ZeroDivisionError:
        return "Cannot divide by zero."

# Using the enhanced divide_numbers function
num1 = float(input("Enter the first number: "))
num2 = float(input("Enter the second number:
"))

result = divide_numbers(num1, num2)
print(f"Result of division: {result}")
```

Explanation:
- The `divide_numbers` function now includes error handling to catch a `ZeroDivisionError`.
- The user is prompted to enter numbers, and the program handles the case where the user attempts to divide by zero.

Chapter 18: Leveling Up - Advanced Python Concepts

Dear maestro of Pythonic symphonies, in this advanced chapter, we ascend to new heights of Pythonic mastery. You'll be introduced to decorators, the stylish embellishments for your functions; generators, where laziness takes center stage; and context managers, because cleanup should be as lazy as the rest of your Pythonic composition.

 # Decorators: The Stylish Embellishments

Decorators are the bow ties and cufflinks of Pythonic functions, adding style and functionality with elegance.

Creating a Decorator

```python
# Creating a simple decorator
def greet_decorator(func):
    def wrapper(*args, **kwargs):
        print("Greetings before the function.")
        result = func(*args, **kwargs)
        print("Greetings after the function.")
        return result
    return wrapper
```

```python
# Applying the decorator
@greet_decorator
def greet(name):
    print(f"Hello, {name}!")

# Invoking the decorated function
greet("Alice")
```

The lazy decorator, `greet_decorator`, dresses up the `greet` function with pre and post greetings.

Generators: Laziness in Action

Generators are lazy performers, producing values on-demand without wasting energy.

Creating a Generator Function

```python
# Creating a generator function
def count_up_to(limit):
    count = 1
    while count <= limit:
        yield count
        count += 1

# Using the generator
for number in count_up_to(5):
    print(number)
```

The lazy generator, `count_up_to`, produces numbers on demand, conserving resources.

Context Managers: Lazy Cleanup

Context managers are the janitors of your Pythonic symphony, ensuring lazy and efficient cleanup.

Creating a Context Manager

```python
# Creating a context manager
class FileManager:
    def __init__(self, filename, mode):
        self.filename = filename
        self.mode = mode

    def __enter__(self):
        self.file = open(self.filename, self.mode)
        return self.file

    def __exit__(self, exc_type, exc_value, traceback):
        self.file.close()

# Using the context manager
with FileManager("my_file.txt", "w") as file:
    file.write("Pythonic cleanliness.")
```

The lazy context manager, `FileManager`, opens and closes the file with finesse.

The Lazy Composer's Guide to Advanced Python Concepts

In our grand finale, embrace these advanced moves for Pythonic mastery:

Decorator with Arguments: The Custom Tailoring

```python
# Creating a decorator with arguments
def repeat(n):
    def decorator(func):
        def wrapper(*args, **kwargs):
            for _ in range(n):
                result = func(*args, **kwargs)
            return result
        return wrapper
    return decorator

# Applying the decorator with arguments
@repeat(3)
def greet(name):
    print(f"Hello, {name}!")
```

The lazy decorator, `repeat`, customizes the function to repeat a specified number of times.

Yielding from Generators: The Collaborative Symphony

```python
# Yielding from multiple generators
def concatenate_generators(gen1, gen2):
    yield from gen1
    yield from gen2

# Using the collaborative generators
```

```
gen1 = count_up_to(3)
gen2 = count_up_to(2)
for number in concatenate_generators(gen1,
gen2):
    print(number)
```

The lazy composer orchestrates a collaborative symphony with multiple generators.

Using the `with` Statement for Context Managers

```
# Using the with statement for a context
manager
with FileManager("my_file.txt", "r") as file:
    content = file.read()
    print(content)
```

The `with` statement conducts the lazy cleanup symphony, ensuring that resources are managed efficiently.

The Pythonic Symphony Reaches New Heights

As we conclude our exploration of advanced Python concepts, you've ascended to new heights of Pythonic mastery. Decorators, generators, and context managers are now integral parts of your symphony, adding style, laziness, and efficient cleanup to your compositions.

The Pythonic symphony, however, is an endless journey. As you continue to compose melodies, may you find inspiration in the elegance of advanced Python concepts. Bravo, Pythonic maestro, and may your symphony resonate through the digital realm with everlasting brilliance!

Examples

Example 1: Creating a Simple Decorator

```python
# Creating a simple decorator
def my_decorator(func):
    def wrapper():
        print("Something is happening before the function is called.")
        func()
        print("Something is happening after the function is called.")
    return wrapper

@my_decorator
def say_hello():
    print("Hello!")

# Using the decorated function
say_hello()
```

Explanation:
- A decorator is a function that wraps another function to enhance or modify its behavior.
- In this example, `my_decorator` adds functionality before and after the original function (`say_hello`) is called.

Example 2: Decorator with Arguments

```python
# Decorator with arguments
def repeat(n):
    def decorator(func):
        def wrapper(*args, **kwargs):
            for _ in range(n):
                func(*args, **kwargs)
        return wrapper
    return decorator

@repeat(3)
def greet(name):
    print(f"Hello, {name}!")

# Using the decorated function
greet("Alice")
```

Explanation:
- Decorators can take arguments, allowing for customization.
- In this example, `repeat` is a decorator factory that creates a decorator to repeat the decorated function a specified number of times.

Example 3: Creating a Simple Generator

```python
# Creating a simple generator
def countdown(n):
    while n > 0:
        yield n
        n -= 1

# Using the generator
```

```
for number in countdown(5):
    print(number)
```

Explanation:
- Generators allow you to create iterators lazily.
- The `yield` statement is used to produce a sequence of values, one at a time.
- In this example, `countdown` generates a countdown sequence.

Example 4: Infinite Generator

```
# Infinite generator
def infinite_sequence():
    num = 0
    while True:
        yield num
        num += 1

# Using the infinite generator
for number in infinite_sequence():
    if number > 10:
        break
    print(number)
```

Explanation:
- Generators can be infinite, allowing you to generate values on-the-fly without storing them in memory.

Example 5: Creating a Context Manager

```python
# Creating a context manager
class MyContext:
    def __enter__(self):
        print("Entering the context.")
        return self  # The object returned by
__enter__ is bound to the variable after 'as'

    def __exit__(self, exc_type, exc_value,
traceback):
        print("Exiting the context.")

# Using the context manager
with MyContext() as context:
    print("Inside the context.")
```

Explanation:
- Context managers allow you to manage resources (like file handling) by defining setup and cleanup actions.
- The `__enter__` method is called when entering the context, and `__exit__` is called when exiting.

Example 6: Using `contextlib` for Simple Context Managers

```python
# Using 'contextlib' for simple context
managers
from contextlib import contextmanager

@contextmanager
def my_context():
    print("Entering the context.")
    yield  # The value yielded by the generator
```

```
is bound to the variable after 'as'
    print("Exiting the context.")

# Using the context manager
with my_context():
    print("Inside the context.")
```

Explanation:
- The `contextlib` module provides utilities for creating context managers with less boilerplate.
- The `@contextmanager` decorator turns a generator function into a context manager.

Chapter 19: Real-world Lazy Projects

Dear Pythonic virtuoso, in this chapter, we embark on a journey to the practical side of laziness. You'll learn how to build real-world lazy projects using Python and discover the art of automating everyday tasks—the true essence of Pythonic elegance.

Building Practical Applications

Project 1: File Organizer

- **Objective:** Create a script that organizes files in a specified directory based on their types (e.g., images, documents, videos).

- **Lazy Approach:** Leverage Python's `os` module to traverse files, classify them by type, and move them to designated folders.

```
# Lazy File Organizer
```

```
import os
import shutil

def organize_files(source_dir):
    for filename in os.listdir(source_dir):
        file_path = os.path.join(source_dir,
filename)

        if os.path.isfile(file_path):
            file_type =
filename.split(".")[-1].lower()
            destination_folder =
os.path.join(source_dir, file_type)

            if not
os.path.exists(destination_folder):
                os.makedirs(destination_folder)

            shutil.move(file_path,
os.path.join(destination_folder, filename))

# Usage
organize_files("/path/to/source/directory")
```

Project 2: Weather Notifier

- **Objective:** Build a script that fetches the current weather for a specified location and sends a notification.

- **Lazy Approach:** Utilize a weather API (e.g., OpenWeatherMap), and a notification library (e.g., `plyer`) to display the weather on the desktop.

```python
# Lazy Weather Notifier
import requests
from plyer import notification

def get_weather(api_key, city):
    url =
f"http://api.openweathermap.org/data/2.5/weathe
r?q={city}&appid={api_key}"
    response = requests.get(url)
    data = response.json()
    weather_description =
data["weather"][0]["description"]
    return f"Weather in {city}:
{weather_description}"

def send_notification(message):
    notification.notify(
        title="Weather Update",
        message=message,
        app_icon=None,    # e.g.,
"path/to/icon.png"
        timeout=10
    )

# Usage
api_key = "your_openweathermap_api_key"
city = "your_city"
weather_message = get_weather(api_key, city)
send_notification(weather_message)
```

Automating Everyday Tasks: The Lazy Way

Task Automation 1: Email Scheduler

- **Objective:** Automate sending recurring emails (e.g., daily reminders, weekly updates).

- **Lazy Approach:** Use the `smtplib` library to send emails at scheduled intervals using Python's `schedule` library.

```python
# Lazy Email Scheduler
import schedule
import smtplib
from email.mime.text import MIMEText

def send_email():
    sender_email = "your_email@gmail.com"
    receiver_email =
"recipient_email@gmail.com"
    subject = "Daily Reminder"
    body = "Don't forget to be awesome today!"

    message = MIMEText(body)
    message["Subject"] = subject
    message["From"] = sender_email
    message["To"] = receiver_email

    with smtplib.SMTP("smtp.gmail.com", 587) as
server:
        server.starttls()
        server.login(sender_email,
"your_email_password")
        server.sendmail(sender_email,
```

```
receiver_email, message.as_string())

# Schedule email every day at 9 AM
schedule.every().day.at("09:00").do(send_email)

while True:
    schedule.run_pending()
```

Task Automation 2: Backup Script

- **Objective:** Automate regular backups of important files to a specified destination.

- **Lazy Approach:** Use the `shutil` library to copy files and schedule the script using a tool like `cron` on Unix or Task Scheduler on Windows.

```
# Lazy Backup Script
import shutil
import schedule

def backup_files(source, destination):
    shutil.copytree(source, destination)

# Schedule backup every Sunday at midnight
schedule.every().sunday.at("00:00").do(backup_f
iles, source="/path/to/important/files",
destination="/path/to/backup/location")

while True:
```

```
schedule.run_pending()
```

The Lazy Composer's Guide to Real-world Projects

In our grand finale, embrace these lazy moves for real-world lazy projects:

Leveraging APIs

```
# Fetching data from a public API
import requests

response =
requests.get("https://api.example.com/data")
data = response.json()
```

GUI Applications

```
# Building a simple GUI app using Tkinter
import tkinter as tk

app = tk.Tk()
app.title("Lazy App")

label = tk.Label(app, text="Hello, Lazy
World!")
label.pack()

app.mainloop()
```

Web Scraping

```
# Web scraping with BeautifulSoup
from bs4 import BeautifulSoup
import requests

url = "https://example.com"
response = requests.get(url)
soup = BeautifulSoup(response.text,
"html.parser")
# Extract information from the HTML soup
```

The Pythonic Symphony Continues to Soar

As we conclude our journey into real-world lazy projects, you've mastered the art of building practical applications and automating everyday tasks with Python. Your Pythonic symphony is now a harmonious blend of creativity, efficiency, and laziness.

The Pythonic symphony, however, is an everlasting melody. As you continue your journey, may your compositions resonate through the digital realm, creating echoes of elegance, simplicity, and the essence of Pythonic laziness. Bravo, Pythonic maestro, and may your symphony play on!

Chapter 20: Becoming a Python Pro

Dear Pythonic virtuoso, in this final chapter, we celebrate your journey from a beginner to a Python Pro. Here, you'll find tips, tricks, and valuable resources for mastering Python, ensuring that your symphony continues to resonate with elegance and expertise.

Tips and Tricks for Mastery

1. **Read Python Source Code:**
   - Dive into the source code of popular Python libraries and frameworks. This not only enhances your understanding but also exposes you to best practices.

2. **Contribute to Open Source:**
   - Contribute to open-source projects. It's a fantastic way to learn, collaborate with experienced developers, and build a professional network.

3. **Use Pythonic Idioms:**
   - Embrace Pythonic idioms and coding styles. Follow PEP 8, Python's style guide, to write clean and readable code.

4. **Explore Advanced Topics:**
   - Delve into advanced topics like decorators, metaclasses, and concurrency. Understanding these concepts elevates your Pythonic compositions.

5. **Master Virtual Environments:**
   - Learn to use virtual environments to manage dependencies. This is crucial for project isolation and maintaining consistent environments.

6. **Practice Regularly:**
   - Practice solving coding challenges on platforms like LeetCode and HackerRank. Consistent practice sharpens your problem-solving skills.

7. **Learn Testing:**

- Master testing frameworks like `unittest` and `pytest`. Writing tests ensures the reliability and maintainability of your code.

8. **Understand Memory Management:**
   - Gain a deep understanding of Python's memory management. Know how objects are allocated and deallocated to write efficient code.

Resources for Continuous Learning

1. **Official Documentation:**
   - The [official Python documentation](https://docs.python.org/3/) is an invaluable resource. It covers everything from language basics to advanced topics.

2. **Online Courses:**
   - Platforms like Stackfoss, Coursera, edX, and Udemy offer comprehensive Python courses. Look for courses from reputable institutions and instructors.

3. **Books:**
   - Explore Python books by renowned authors such as "Fluent Python" by Luciano Ramalho and "Effective Python" by Brett Slatkin.

4. **Podcasts:**
   - Stay updated with Python podcasts like "Talk Python to Me" and "Python Bytes" to hear discussions on trends, tools, and best practices.

5. **Community Participation:**

- Join forums like StackOverflow and the Python community on Reddit. Engage in discussions, ask questions, and share your knowledge.

6. **Conferences and Meetups:**
   - Attend Python conferences and local meetups. These events provide opportunities to learn from experts and network with fellow enthusiasts.

7. **Newsletters:**
   - Subscribe to newsletters like "Python Weekly" to receive curated updates, tutorials, and articles directly in your inbox.

Celebrating the Journey

As we celebrate your journey from a Python novice to a seasoned pro, remember that mastery is a continuous process. Embrace the joy of learning, stay curious, and never shy away from exploring new corners of the Pythonic landscape.

Your journey doesn't end here; it evolves. As a Python Pro, you are now part of a vibrant community shaping the future of technology. Bravo, Pythonic maestro, and may your symphony play on with everlasting brilliance!

Appendices

A. Quick Reference Guide for Python Syntax

1. Variables and Data Types

- **Variable Assignment:**

```
x = 10
name = "Alice"
```

- **Common Data Types:**
```
num = 3.14    # float
count = 42     # int
message = "Hello, Python!"   # str
```

2. Control Flow

- **If Statement:**
```
if x > 5:
    print("x is greater than 5")
```

- **For Loop:**
```
for item in my_list:
    print(item)
```

- **While Loop:**
```
while condition:
    print("Still running")
```

3. Functions

- **Function Definition:**
```
def greet(name):
    return f"Hello, {name}!"
```

- **Function Call:**

```
result = greet("Alice")
```

4. Lists and Dictionaries

- **List:**
```
my_list = [1, 2, 3, 4, 5]
```

- **Dictionary:**
```
my_dict = {"name": "Alice", "age": 30}
```

5. Classes and Objects

- **Class Definition:**
```
class Dog:
    def bark(self):
        print("Woof!")
```

- **Object Creation:**
```
my_dog = Dog()
```

6. Exception Handling

- **Try, Except, Finally:**
```
try:
    result = 10 / 0
except ZeroDivisionError:
    print("Cannot divide by zero.")
finally:
```

```
    print("Cleanup")
```

B. Troubleshooting Common Lazy Mistakes

1. Indentation Errors

- **Lazy Mistake:**
```
  def my_function():
  print("Hello")
```

- **Fix:**
```
 def my_function():
      print("Hello")
```

2. Forgetting Colons in Control Flow

- **Lazy Mistake:**
```
 if x > 5
      print("x is greater than 5")
```

- **Fix:**
```
 if x > 5:
      print("x is greater than 5")
```

3. Incorrect Variable Names

- **Lazy Mistake:**
```
 X = 10
```

- **Fix:**

```
x = 10
```

4. Mismatched Parentheses

- **Lazy Mistake:**

```
result = add_numbers(2, 3
```

- **Fix:**

```
result = add_numbers(2, 3)
```

C. Glossary for Lazy Programmers

1. Pythonic:

- *Definition:* Adhering to the principles and idioms of the Python programming language for clean, readable, and elegant code.

2. Zen of Python:

- *Definition:* A collection of guiding principles for writing computer programs in Python, written by Tim Peters.

3. Decorator:

- *Definition:* A design pattern in Python that allows the modification of functions or methods using a higher-order function.

4. Pythonista:

- *Definition:* An enthusiastic and skilled practitioner of Python programming.

5. PEP 8:

- *Definition:* Python Enhancement Proposal 8 is the style guide for Python code. It provides conventions for writing readable and consistent code.

6. Lazy Evaluation:

- *Definition:* An evaluation strategy that delays the evaluation of an expression until its value is actually needed.

7. Python Package Index (PyPI):

- *Definition:* A repository of software packages for Python. pip, the package installer for Python, installs packages from PyPI.

8. Magic Methods:

- *Definition:* Special methods in Python that start and end with double underscores (e.g., `__init__`). They are used for operator overloading and other special behaviors.

9. Bytecode:

- *Definition:* Intermediate code that is generated by the Python interpreter from the source code and executed by the Python Virtual Machine (PVM).

10. Generator:

- *Definition:* A special kind of iterator in Python that allows lazy evaluation. Generators are created using functions with the `yield` keyword.

D. Further Reading and Resources

- Python Documentation: Official Python documentation for in-depth information on language features and modules.